THE YOUNG MONEY BLUEPRINT

A Young Hustler's Guide to Financial Freedom and Building an Empire

Kim Domingo Reyes

KIM DOMINGOREYES

No part of this book may be reproduced or transmitted in any form whatsoever, electronic, or mechanical, including photocopying, recording, or by any informational storage or retrieval system without express permission from the author or publisher.

Copyright © 2024 RJK Publishing
All rights reserved

INTRODUCTION

Picture this: You're not stressing over bills, you can book that spontaneous weekend trip with friends, or you can invest in your passion project without worrying about the price tag. That's the beauty of financial freedom. It's about having the resources to say "yes" to the things that truly matter to you, and "no" to the things that don't.

Think of it like this: money is the fuel, but financial freedom is the destination. It's the ability to create the life you want, filled with experiences that light you up and opportunities to make a difference in the world.

Designing Your Dream Life: Start Now, Not After Graduation

The beauty of being young is that you have a blank canvas in front of you. Don't wait until you're out of school or stuck in a dead-end job to start dreaming big. Start now. What kind of life do you envision for yourself? Do you see yourself traveling the world, building a tech empire, or becoming a renowned artist?

Grab a notebook (or open a note on your phone) and start brainstorming. Write down your wildest dreams, your deepest desires, and the things that make you feel truly alive. This is your vision board for the future, and it's never too early to start creating it.

In the realm of life and success, a pivotal debate has emerged, pitting school smarts against money smarts. While academic achievements hold their own significance, the truth is that grades alone do not determine one's financial future. In fact, the correlation between academic excellence and financial success is often tenuous at best.

Traditional education systems, while rigorous and comprehensive, often fail to equip students with the practical financial skills essential for navigating the complexities of the real world. School curriculums emphasize subjects such as mathematics, science, history, and literature, but fail to provide adequate exposure to personal finance, investment, and entrepreneurship. As a result, many individuals graduate with impressive degrees but lack the financial literacy needed to make sound financial decisions.

The world of business and finance operates on a different set of principles than academia. In the arena of entrepreneurship, creativity, adaptability, risk-taking, and a keen understanding of market dynamics are often more valuable than a straight-A report card. Many successful entrepreneurs, such as Bill Gates, Steve Jobs, and Mark Zuckerberg, were not stellar students, yet they managed to build multi-billion dollar empires through their innovative ideas and exceptional business acumen.

This is not to downplay the importance of education. A solid academic foundation provides critical thinking skills, analytical abilities, and a thirst for knowledge. However, it is crucial to recognize that school smarts alone are insufficient for financial success. To truly excel in the world of finance, individuals need to acquire practical money management skills, such as budgeting, saving, investing, and debt management.

Financial education should start at a young age, preferably during the formative years of schooling. By incorporating financial literacy into the educational curriculum, students can develop a solid foundation for making informed financial decisions throughout their lives. Topics such as compound interest, the power of saving, and the basics of investing should be introduced to students at an early age, fostering a mindset of financial responsibility and long-term planning.

Moreover, individuals need to take an active role in their own financial education. There are numerous resources available, both online and offline, that can provide valuable insights into personal finance, investing, and entrepreneurship. By continuously seeking knowledge and applying it to their financial lives, individuals can empower themselves to make informed decisions, build wealth, and achieve financial freedom.

In conclusion, while school smarts are important, they are not the sole determinant of one's financial future. To achieve true financial success, individuals need to possess a combination of academic knowledge, practical financial skills, and a mindset geared towards financial growth. By investing in their financial education and taking control of their financial decisions, individuals can unlock their full potential and pave the way for a financially secure and fulfilling life.

DEEPER DEFINITION OF FINANCIAL FREEDOM

Financial freedom is often heralded as the ultimate goal for many aspiring entrepreneurs, investors, and individuals seeking a life of autonomy and choice. But what does financial freedom truly entail, and how can it serve as your ticket to living life on your terms? Let's embark on an in-depth exploration of this concept, dissecting its components, implications, and the pathways to achieving it.

At its core, financial freedom is the state of having sufficient personal wealth to live, without having to work actively for basic necessities. It means your assets generate income that exceeds your expenses. However, this definition barely scratches the surface. Financial freedom is not merely a numerical milestone; it's a transformative journey that offers unparalleled choices, experiences, and the power to impact your world and that of others positively.

The Layers of Financial Freedom

Economic Independence: The first layer involves reaching a point where you no longer live paycheck to paycheck. Your savings buffer allows you to comfortably manage your expenses and afford some luxuries without incurring debt.

Sustainable Wealth: Beyond mere independence, sustainable wealth involves investments, assets, and passive income streams that not only cover your current lifestyle but also grow over time, outpacing inflation and taxation.

Autonomy of Time: True financial freedom grants you the autonomy of time. It's about having the freedom to choose how, where, and on what you spend your time, whether it's on personal development, hobbies, or philanthropy.

Freedom of Choice: With financial barriers removed, you gain the freedom to make choices that align with your deepest values and desires, from pursuing passions to changing careers or starting a business.

Legacy Building: Ultimately, financial freedom allows for the creation and perpetuation of a legacy. This could mean providing for future generations, contributing to causes you care about, or leaving a tangible mark on the world.

Achieving Financial Freedom

Achieving financial freedom requires a multifaceted approach, encompassing mindset, strategy, and execution.

Mindset

The journey begins with a mindset shift. Understanding that financial freedom is possible and cultivating a positive relationship with money is foundational. It's about seeing money as a tool for creating the life you want and recognizing that disciplined, informed financial decisions lead to greater autonomy.

Strategy

Income Diversification: Don't rely solely on a single source of income. Explore avenues to diversify your income through investments, side hustles, and passive income streams.

Savings and Investments: Prioritize saving a significant portion of your income, and invest wisely. It's not just about saving money, but about putting your money to work for you through investments in stocks, bonds, real estate, or businesses.

Expenditure Management: Achieving financial freedom isn't solely about making more money; it's equally about managing your expenses. Adopting a lifestyle that balances enjoyment today with financial goals for tomorrow is key.

Financial Education: Continuously educate yourself on financial matters. Understanding the basics of personal finance, investment strategies, and economic principles can empower your decision-making process.

Risk Management: Protecting your assets through insurance, and having an emergency fund, ensures that unforeseen events don't derail your journey towards financial freedom.

Execution

Consistency is paramount. Regularly review your financial plan, adjust your strategies as necessary, and stay committed to your long-term vision. Remember, financial freedom is not achieved overnight but through years of disciplined effort and smart financial choices.

Financial freedom is much more than attaining wealth; it's about building a life rich in experiences, choices, and contributions. It demands a comprehensive approach that encompasses changing your mindset towards money, implementing robust financial strategies, and executing your plan with discipline and adaptability.

By embracing this journey, not only do you unlock the potential to live life on your terms, but you also gain the opportunity to create a lasting impact. Financial freedom, therefore, is not just your ticket to a fulfilling life; it's a pathway to leaving a meaningful legacy.

OVERCOMING THE FEAR OF FAILURE AND SELF-DOUBT

The fear of failure is a powerful force that can hold young entrepreneurs back from reaching their full potential. This fear can manifest in many ways, such as:

- Worrying that your idea won't be good enough.
- Being afraid of losing money.
- Fearing being laughed at or criticized.
- Feeling overwhelmed by the challenges involved in starting a business.

It's important to recognize that the fear of failure is a normal part of the entrepreneurial journey. However, it's crucial not to let this fear paralyze you and prevent you from taking action.

Successful entrepreneurs understand that failure is a natural part of the learning process. They don't let setbacks discourage them; instead, they learn from their mistakes and keep moving forward.

Here are a few tips on how to overcome the fear of failure:

- **Reframe your thinking.** Instead of seeing failure as something to be avoided, view it as an opportunity to learn and grow. Every failure brings you one step closer to success.
- **Focus on your strengths.** Everyone has unique strengths and weaknesses. When you're feeling doubtful, focus on your strengths and what you can contribute to your

business.
- **Take small steps.** Don't try to do everything at once. Break down your goals into smaller, more manageable steps. This will help you feel less overwhelmed and more confident in your ability to succeed.
- **Seek support.** Surround yourself with a supportive network of friends, family, and mentors who can offer encouragement and advice when you need it most.
- **Celebrate your successes.** When you achieve a goal, no matter how small, take the time to celebrate your success. This will help you build confidence and motivation.

Remember, failure is not the opposite of success; it's a part of it. Embrace your failures as learning opportunities and use them to fuel your growth. And when self-doubt creeps in, remind yourself of all the incredible things you're capable of.

Young and Limitless: Busting the Age Myth

Who says you have to wait until you're "grown up" to start making serious money? Newsflash: the world is changing, and age is becoming less and less relevant when it comes to entrepreneurial success.

Teen Tycoons: Real-Life Examples of Young Entrepreneurs Who Made It Big

Let's take a look at some inspiring examples of young entrepreneurs who are already making waves:

- **Mikaila Ulmer:** Started her own lemonade business at age 4 and now has a multi-million dollar company.
- **Hart Main:** Launched a successful clothing line at age 13 and is now a social media influencer.
- **Moziah Bridges:** Founded his own bow tie company at age 9 and has been featured on Shark Tank.

These are just a few examples of young people who didn't let their age hold them back. They saw an opportunity, took action, and built successful businesses while still in school.

In the realm of entrepreneurship, where innovation and adaptability are paramount, youth offers a unique set of competitive advantages. Here's how tech fluency, fresh perspectives, and the element of surprise can give you an edge:

Tech Fluency:

- **Digital Proficiency:** Having grown up in the digital age, you possess an innate understanding of technology. You effortlessly navigate smartphones, social media, and the internet, essential skills for any contemporary business.
- **Adaptability to New Tech:** Your comfort with technology makes you adaptable to emerging trends. You can quickly learn new platforms and tools, staying ahead of the curve in a rapidly evolving digital landscape.
- **Innovative Thinking:** Your familiarity with technology can lead to innovative ideas and solutions. You can merge different technologies or apply them in unconventional ways, unlocking new possibilities.

Fresh Perspectives:

- **Challenging the Status Quo:** Unburdened by traditional mindsets, you're unafraid to question established norms and practices. This enables you to identify inefficiencies and propose creative solutions that might elude others.
- **Unconventional Approaches:** Your openness to new ideas allows you to think outside the box. You can explore alternative business models, marketing strategies, or product designs that may surprise and delight your customers.
- **Adaptability to Change:** In a constantly evolving business environment, your willingness to embrace change is a valuable asset. You can quickly pivot your strategies, products, or services to meet evolving market demands.

Element of Surprise:

- **Underestimated Potential:** People often underestimate young entrepreneurs, which can work to your advantage. Use this to your benefit by exceeding expectations and proving them wrong.
- **Unpredictability:** Your unconventional approaches and fresh perspectives can catch competitors off guard. This element of surprise can give you a tactical advantage in the market.
- **Reputation-Building:** When you consistently deliver beyond expectations, your reputation as a reliable and innovative entrepreneur grows, attracting customers, partners, and investors.

By leveraging your tech fluency, fresh perspectives, and the element of surprise, you can gain a competitive edge in the entrepreneurial world. Embrace your unique advantages and use them to chart a path to success.

Overcoming Doubts: How to Silence the Naysayers (Including Yourself)

It's inevitable that you'll encounter doubters along your entrepreneurial journey. Some might be well-meaning friends or family members who are simply concerned about your future. Others might be jealous or simply don't believe in your vision.

The most important thing is to not let their doubts discourage you. Surround yourself with positive and supportive people who believe in your dreams. And when those negative thoughts creep into your own mind, remind yourself of all the reasons why you're capable of achieving great things.

Building Confidence and Resilience

Building confidence is like building a muscle; it takes time and effort. Start by setting small goals and celebrating your wins, no matter how small. As you rack up accomplishments, your confidence will naturally grow.

Resilience is the ability to bounce back from setbacks and keep moving forward. It's an essential trait for any entrepreneur, as the road to success is rarely smooth. Develop your resilience by embracing challenges as learning opportunities and refusing to give up on your dreams.

Think Like a CEO, Not a Consumer

In this pivotal chapter, we delve into the mindset shift required to succeed as an entrepreneur. It's time to shed the consumer mentality and embrace the responsibilities and opportunities that come with being a CEO. Taking ownership of your financial future, making strategic decisions, and building a solid foundation for your business are paramount to achieving entrepreneurial success.

The Broke Student Trap: How to Avoid the Debt Cycle and Build Wealth Early

Many young people, eager to pursue higher education, fall into the trap of accumulating substantial debt through student loans, credit card spending, and impulsive purchases. This financial burden can have lasting effects, hindering their ability to invest in their future and pursue entrepreneurial ventures.

To avoid this pitfall, it's essential to cultivate healthy financial habits early on. Create a comprehensive budget that tracks your income and expenses. This will help you identify areas where you can cut back on unnecessary spending and allocate more funds towards savings and investments. Consider getting a part-time job or starting a side hustle to supplement your income and build your financial foundation.

The Power of Mindset: Shifting from Scarcity to Abundance

Your mindset plays a crucial role in determining your financial success. If you hold a scarcity mindset, believing that money is limited and that financial struggles are inevitable, it can become a self-fulfilling prophecy.

Instead, cultivate an abundance mindset. Embrace the belief that there are limitless opportunities to create wealth and that you deserve financial prosperity. This positive mindset can open doors to new possibilities, attract abundance into your life, and empower you to take calculated risks in your entrepreneurial journey.

MANAGING FINANCES AND BUDGETING

Financial freedom begins with understanding how to manage your money effectively. It's not about penny-pinching but about being intentional and strategic with your financial decisions.

Track Your Spending: Gain clarity on where your money is going by using budgeting apps or spreadsheets. This will help you identify areas where you can cut back and reallocate funds towards your financial goals.

Create a Budget: Develop a budget that aligns with your financial objectives. Allocate a portion of your income towards savings, investments, and essential expenses, ensuring that your spending aligns with your long-term vision.

Save and Invest: Make saving a habit by setting aside a percentage of your income each month. Explore investment options such as stocks, bonds, mutual funds, or real estate to grow your wealth over time.

Avoid Debt: Debt can be a significant obstacle to financial freedom. Avoid unnecessary debt, such as credit card debt or high-interest loans, and focus on building assets instead of liabilities.

UNDERSTANDING TAXES AND LEGAL REQUIREMENTS

Taxes and legal requirements are integral aspects of running a business. It's essential to have a basic understanding of the tax implications of your entrepreneurial activities and to comply with all legal obligations.

Learn the Basics: Familiarize yourself with different types of taxes that might apply to your business, such as income tax, sales tax, and self-employment tax. Consult a tax professional if you need assistance or have specific questions.

Consult a Professional: Seeking advice from a tax professional or lawyer can be invaluable. They can help you navigate complex tax laws and ensure that your business is compliant with all legal requirements.

Stay Compliant: Staying compliant with tax laws and regulations is crucial to avoid legal complications and ensure the long-term sustainability of your venture.

By embracing the mindset of a CEO, developing healthy financial habits, and understanding the fundamentals of managing finances and legal requirements, you'll lay a solid foundation for your entrepreneurial journey. This knowledge and skill set will empower you to make informed decisions, seize opportunities, and create a financially successful and fulfilling life.

The Side Hustle Revolution: Making Money on Your Terms

In a world where the traditional 9-to-5 job feels increasingly outdated, teenagers are embracing the side hustles - flexible, creative ways to make money that align with their schedule and passions. No longer limited to the lemonade stand, today's teens are exploring the endless opportunities of the digital age.

Social Media Mogul: Monetizing Your Online Presence

For the social media-savvy teen, monetizing your online presence is a no-brainer. Social media isn't just a platform for sharing memes and selfies; it's a powerful tool for building a personal brand and generating income.

1. **Influencer Marketing:**
   - If you have a talent for creating engaging content and building a loyal following, brands might be eager to pay you to promote their products or services.
   - Collaborate with brands that align with your values and interests, ensuring authenticity in your promotions.
2. **Affiliate Marketing:**
   - Partner with companies to promote their products through your unique referral link.
   - Earn a commission on each sale made through your link, providing a passive income stream.
   - Choose products or services that you genuinely believe in and would recommend to your followers.
3. **Content Creation:**
   - Create and sell digital products such as e-books, online courses, or templates on platforms like Etsy or Gumroad.
   - Share your expertise, passions, or creative talents with the world and earn money while doing what you love.
4. **Social Media Management:**
   - Offer your social media expertise to businesses that lack the time or resources to manage their online

presence effectively.
- Provide services such as content creation, scheduling, community engagement, and analytics reporting.

The Gig Economy: Unleashing Your Entrepreneurial Spirit

The gig economy presents a transformative opportunity for individuals seeking financial flexibility and entrepreneurial pursuits. By harnessing the power of technology and platforms, anyone can turn everyday tasks and passions into profitable business ventures.

Food Delivery:

- Partner with food delivery services like DoorDash and Uber Eats to deliver meals to customers' doorsteps.
- Leverage meal planning and route optimization apps to maximize efficiency and earnings.
- Offer customized services, such as contactless delivery or special dietary accommodations.

Dog Walking/Pet Sitting:

- Register with platforms like Rover and Wag to provide dog walking and pet sitting services.
- Build a loyal client base by offering personalized care and regular updates.
- Expand your services to include pet grooming, training, or transportation.

Tutoring:

- Share your knowledge and expertise by offering tutoring services in subjects you excel at.
- Utilize online platforms like Wyzant and TutorMe to connect with students in need of academic support.
- Tailor your tutoring sessions to meet the individual needs of each student.

Errand Running/TaskRabbit:

- Offer a variety of errand-running services, such as grocery shopping, dry cleaning, or package delivery.
- Utilize task management apps to streamline your workflow and optimize your time.
- Build relationships with local businesses to offer exclusive services or discounts to your clients.

Unlocking Your Hidden Talents: Monetizing Your Passions

Your passions hold the key to unlocking your entrepreneurial potential. Transform your hobbies and interests into profitable ventures by exploring these avenues:

Sell Your Art or Crafts:

- Create an online store on platforms like Etsy or Shopify to showcase and sell your artwork, crafts, or handmade goods.
- Promote your products through social media, email marketing, and influencer collaborations.
- Offer custom commissions and personalized creations to meet the unique desires of your customers.

Offer Freelance Services:

- Utilize freelance platforms like Upwork and Fiverr to offer your skills in writing, editing, graphic design, or web development.
- Build a strong portfolio to showcase your work and attract potential clients.
- Network with other freelancers and industry professionals to expand your reach.

Create and Sell Digital Products:

- Turn your knowledge and expertise into digital products like e-books, online courses, or downloadable templates.
- Leverage platforms like Amazon Kindle Direct Publishing (KDP) and Teachable to distribute and sell your digital products globally.

- Provide ongoing support and updates to your customers to ensure their satisfaction.

Teach Online Classes:

- Share your skills and knowledge by teaching online classes or workshops through platforms like Skillshare and Udemy.
- Create engaging and informative content that meets the needs of your target audience.
- Promote your online classes through social media, email marketing, and online communities.

Finding Work-Life Balance

While side hustles offer flexibility and freedom, it's important to maintain a healthy work-life balance. Don't let your entrepreneurial pursuits consume all your time and energy.

- **Set Boundaries:** Establish clear boundaries between your work and personal life. Set specific work hours and stick to them.
- **Schedule Time for Yourself:** Make time for activities you enjoy, whether it's spending time with friends, pursuing hobbies, or simply relaxing.
- **Prioritize Your Health:** Don't neglect your physical and mental health. Make sure you're getting enough sleep, exercise, and healthy food.

HIGH-INCOME SKILLS FOR THE DIGITAL AGE

In the digital age, certain skills are in high demand and can command a premium salary. By mastering these skills, you can set yourself up for financial success and open doors to exciting career opportunities.

In today's digital age, coding is not just a technical skill but a gateway to lucrative career opportunities. With coding, individuals can build websites, develop apps, and create software solutions that drive innovation and shape the digital landscape. Here's an expanded elaboration of the input text:

Coding for Cash: Building Websites, Apps, and Software Solutions

1. The Demand for Coding Skills:
- Coding is the foundation of the digital economy, and demand for skilled coders continues to soar.
- From e-commerce platforms to mobile applications, coding skills are essential for creating and maintaining the technological infrastructure of businesses and organizations worldwide.

2. Career Opportunities in Coding:
- **Web Developers:** Create and maintain websites, ensuring their functionality, usability, and visual appeal.
- **App Developers:** Design and develop mobile applications for

various platforms like iOS and Android.
- **Software Engineers:** Build and maintain complex software systems and applications for businesses and industries.
- **Data Scientists:** Use coding skills to analyze and interpret large datasets, providing valuable insights for decision-making.

3. **Learning the Basics of Coding:**

- Start by understanding the fundamentals of coding concepts like variables, data types, functions, and control flow.
- Choose a programming language to focus on, such as Python, JavaScript, or Java, and explore its syntax and semantics.
- Utilize online resources, tutorials, and interactive coding platforms to grasp the basics of coding.

4. **Building Projects to Enhance Skills:**

- Engage in hands-on coding projects to solidify your understanding and apply your skills practically.
- Build a simple website, create a mobile app, or develop a game to showcase your coding abilities.
- Document your projects and include them in your portfolio to demonstrate your proficiency and creativity.

5. **Freelancing and Internships:**

- Gain real-world experience and expand your network by freelancing your coding services or seeking internships in tech companies.
- Work on freelance projects or collaborate with startups to contribute to their coding needs.
- Internships offer valuable opportunities to learn from experienced professionals and contribute to meaningful projects.

6. **Continuous Learning and Specialization:**

- Stay updated with the latest coding trends, frameworks, and technologies to remain competitive.
- Pursue certifications or specialized courses in areas of interest, such as cybersecurity, machine learning, or cloud computing.
- Attend coding workshops, conferences, and meetups to connect with fellow coders and expand your knowledge.

7. Building a Successful Career in Coding:

- Develop your problem-solving, analytical, and critical thinking skills to excel as a coder.
- Maintain a strong portfolio of your coding projects, showcasing your skills and versatility.
- Network with professionals in the tech industry, attend industry events, and participate in coding communities to enhance your career prospects.

Conclusion: Coding for cash is not just a means of earning a living but a rewarding career path that offers opportunities for growth, creativity, and continuous learning. By mastering coding skills, individuals can build websites, develop apps, and create software solutions that shape the digital landscape and positively impact the world.

Digital marketing has revolutionized how businesses connect with their customers. It encompasses a wide range of strategies to promote products or services online. Let's delve deeper into three key areas of digital marketing mastery: Search Engine Optimization (SEO), Social Media Ads, and Content Creation.

1. **SEO (Search Engine Optimization):**
    - Optimizing websites for higher search engine rankings, increasing organic traffic.
    - Conducting keyword research to identify relevant search terms.
    - Creating high-quality content that aligns with search

intent.
- Building backlinks from reputable websites to enhance authority.
- Monitoring website performance and implementing improvements.

2. **Social Media Ads:**
   - Designing and executing targeted advertising campaigns on platforms like Facebook, Instagram, and Twitter.
   - Segmenting audiences based on demographics, interests, and behaviors.
   - Crafting compelling ad copy and visuals to capture attention.
   - Monitoring ad performance and optimizing campaigns for better results.
   - Utilizing social media analytics to gain insights into audience engagement.

3. **Content Creation:**
   - Developing engaging content that resonates with the target audience.
   - Creating blog posts, articles, videos, and social media posts.
   - Utilizing storytelling techniques to connect with readers or viewers.
   - Optimizing content for search engines and social media platforms.
   - Promoting content through multiple channels for maximum reach.

Digital marketing mastery requires a combination of technical skills, creativity, and strategic thinking. By excelling in these three areas, businesses can establish a strong online presence, attract targeted traffic, and achieve their marketing goals.

In the realm of commerce, salesmanship stands as a linchpin, propelling businesses toward success. Regardless of the nature of the product or service—be it lemonade or intricate software—the art of persuasion and influence remains an invaluable skill. Mastering this skill empowers individuals to forge connections, secure deals, and ultimately drive business growth.

At the heart of effective salesmanship lies a profound understanding of the customer. Delving into the psyche of your target audience is crucial. Identifying their deepest pain points and aspirations provides a roadmap for tailoring your approach and resonating with their needs. Empathy becomes your guiding star as you seek to forge an emotional connection, building rapport that lays the foundation for trust and credibility.

With rapport firmly established, the stage is set to present the value proposition. Clearly articulating the benefits of your product or service becomes paramount. Showcase how your offering addresses their challenges, alleviates their pain points, and propels them toward their goals. Every word, every gesture, and every piece of information should be meticulously aligned to highlight the unique value you bring to the table.

However, the path to a successful sale is rarely devoid of obstacles. Anticipating and skillfully handling objections becomes a crucial aspect of the sales process. Objections, when encountered, should be embraced as opportunities to further demonstrate your understanding of the customer's concerns and reinforce the value of your offering. By providing tailored responses that address their apprehensions and reaffirm the benefits they stand to gain, you can effectively navigate objections and keep the sales momentum alive.

Finally, the moment of truth arrives—closing the deal. This delicate phase requires a blend of finesse and determination. Guiding your customers toward a purchase decision involves creating a sense of urgency, emphasizing the limited availability of your product or service, and leveraging social proof to instill confidence in their choice. By skillfully employing these tactics, you can gently nudge your customers toward taking the final step —making a purchase that will not only benefit them but also contribute to the growth and success of your business.

INVESTING FOR THE FUTURE: STOCKS, CRYPTO, AND OTHER OPTIONS FOR YOUNG PEOPLE

Investing can be a strong way to build your wealth over time. While it might seem daunting at first, many resources are available to help you get started. Here are some detailed and popular investment options:

1. Stocks

- **What It Is**: When you buy stocks, you're purchasing ownership in a company. Each share represents a small portion of the company.
- **Why It's Good**: As the company grows and becomes more profitable, the value of your shares can increase, leading to potential gains. Additionally, some companies pay dividends, which are portions of the profit distributed to shareholders.
- **Example**: If you buy shares in a tech company like Apple, and Apple continues to innovate and grow, your shares may increase in value.
- **Tips**:
  - **Research**: Understand the company's business model,

financial health, and industry position.
- o **Diversify**: Don't put all your money into one stock; spread your investments across various sectors.

2. Cryptocurrencies

- **What It Is**: Cryptocurrencies are digital or virtual currencies that use cryptography for security. Bitcoin and Ethereum are among the most well-known.
- **Why It's Good**: Cryptocurrencies have shown significant growth in value over short periods, offering the potential for high returns.
- **Risks**: They are highly volatile and can experience significant price swings in short periods. Regulatory changes and security issues also pose risks.
- **Example**: Bitcoin's value has fluctuated dramatically over the years, offering opportunities for high returns but also posing significant risks.
- **Tips**:
  - o **Stay Informed**: Follow news and trends in the crypto market.
  - o **Risk Management**: Only invest money you can afford to lose due to its volatile nature.

3. Index Funds

- **What It Is**: Index funds are types of mutual funds or ETFs that aim to replicate the performance of a specific index, like the S&P 500.
- **Why It's Good**: They offer broad market exposure, low operating expenses, and low portfolio turnover. Because they are diversified across many stocks, they reduce individual stock risk.
- **Example**: Investing in an S&P 500 index fund means you're investing in 500 of the largest companies in the U.S., spreading out your risk.
- **Tips**:
  - o **Long-Term Investment**: Ideal for those who prefer a

hands-off approach and are looking for steady growth over time.
- o **Low Costs**: Look for funds with low expense ratios to maximize your returns.

4. Real Estate

- **What It Is**: Investing in real estate involves purchasing property to generate income or appreciate in value. This can be done directly by buying property or indirectly through REITs (Real Estate Investment Trusts).
- **Why It's Good**: Real estate can provide steady rental income and potential appreciation over time. It also offers diversification beyond traditional stocks and bonds.
- **Example**: Buying a rental property can generate monthly rental income, while owning shares in a REIT can provide dividends and exposure to the real estate market without the need to manage property directly.
- **Tips**:
  - o **Location Matters**: Invest in areas with strong rental demand and potential for property value appreciation.
  - o **Understand Costs**: Be aware of both upfront costs (like down payments) and ongoing costs (like maintenance and property management).

Final Thoughts

Each investment option comes with its own set of benefits and risks. It's essential to align your investment choices with your financial goals, risk tolerance, and time horizon. Don't rush into any investment without doing thorough research and possibly consulting with a financial advisor. Taking these steps can help you build a diversified portfolio that supports your long-term financial success.

ACQUIRING NECESSARY SKILLS (MARKETING, SALES, FINANCE, ETC.)

In today's digital age, having a solid foundation in essential skills such as marketing, sales, and finance is crucial for entrepreneurs seeking to thrive. Fortunately, there are numerous resources available to help individuals acquire these skills.

Online Learning Platforms:

- **Coursera, Udemy, and Skillshare:** These platforms offer a vast collection of courses on various topics, including marketing, sales, finance, and entrepreneurship. With flexible learning schedules and affordable pricing, these platforms make it convenient for individuals to learn at their own pace.
- **LinkedIn Learning:** LinkedIn's online learning platform provides a comprehensive library of courses taught by industry experts. It also offers personalized recommendations based on your profile and career goals.
- **HubSpot Academy:** This platform offers free online courses and certifications in marketing, sales, and customer service. HubSpot Academy's courses are designed to be practical and applicable to real-world scenarios.

Books and Blogs:

- **Books by Successful Entrepreneurs:** Reading books written by successful entrepreneurs can provide valuable insights into their strategies and experiences. Some recommended books include "The Lean Startup" by Eric Ries, "Traction" by Gabriel Weinberg and Justin Mares, and "Good Strategy/Bad Strategy" by Richard Rumelt.
- **Industry Blogs:** Following industry blogs and publications can keep you updated on the latest trends, best practices, and case studies. Some popular blogs include "MarketingProfs," "Salesforce Blog," and "Harvard Business Review."

Mentorship and Networking:

- **Seek Mentors:** Reach out to experienced entrepreneurs or professionals in your field who can provide guidance and support. Mentors can offer valuable advice, share their experiences, and help you navigate challenges.
- **Attend Industry Events:** Attending conferences, workshops, and networking events is a great way to connect with other entrepreneurs, learn about new trends, and find potential business partners or clients.
- **Join Online Communities:** Participate in online communities and forums related to your field. These platforms offer opportunities to engage in discussions, ask questions, and share your own insights.

By investing time and effort in acquiring essential skills and knowledge, entrepreneurs can increase their chances of success and achieve their business goals. Continuous learning and a commitment to personal and professional development are key factors in building a successful and sustainable enterprise.

LAUNCHING YOUR FIRST VENTURE: NO MONEY, NO PROBLEM

In the realm of entrepreneurship, transforming a brilliant idea into a flourishing business venture often requires more than just passion and determination. Most young entrepreneurs, brimming with potential but lacking substantial financial resources, find themselves at a crossroads. Fear not, for bootstrapping, the art of starting a business with minimal external funding, offers a viable path to success.

Bootstrapping demands resourcefulness, creativity, and an unwavering spirit. It calls for starting small, focusing on manageable projects that can be launched promptly and at a low cost. Keeping expenses in check is paramount, achieved through measures such as working from home, utilizing free or budget-friendly tools, and bartering skills or services whenever possible.

Funding the venture is a crucial aspect of bootstrapping. Exploring alternative options beyond traditional bank loans is essential. Crowdfunding platforms, pre-selling products or services, and seeking microloans from organizations dedicated to supporting young entrepreneurs are viable avenues to consider.

Revenue generation should be the primary objective. Prioritizing activities that directly contribute to income is vital.

Entrepreneurs must steer clear of vanity metrics and unnecessary expenditures that may hinder financial growth.

The lean startup methodology offers a strategic approach to validating business ideas before committing significant resources. It entails testing assumptions, gathering feedback from potential customers, and iteratively refining the product or service based on the insights gained.

Building a minimum viable product (MVP) serves as the foundation of the lean startup methodology. An MVP is a rudimentary version of the product or service, sufficient for market testing. This could be a simple landing page, a prototype, or a beta version of an app.

Feedback is the lifeblood of the lean startup process. Sharing the MVP with potential customers and collecting their feedback is crucial. This feedback provides valuable insights into what resonates with customers, what needs improvement, and what features are essential.

The iterative process of gathering feedback, refining the product or service, and testing again forms the core of the lean startup methodology. Entrepreneurs continuously iterate and improve their offerings until they develop a product that customers are eager to pay for.

Bootstrapping and the lean startup methodology empower aspiring entrepreneurs to turn their innovative ideas into successful ventures, even with limited financial resources. By embracing resourcefulness, creativity, and a data-driven approach, entrepreneurs can navigate the challenges of starting and scaling their businesses effectively.

LEGAL ESSENTIALS FOR YOUNG ENTREPRENEURS: PROTECTING YOUR IDEAS AND AVOIDING LEGAL TROUBLE

As a young entrepreneur, understanding the legal aspects of starting and running a business is crucial for your venture's success. Here's an expanded version of the input text:

1. Choosing the Right Business Structure:

- **Sole Proprietorship**: You're the sole owner and operator, with complete control and responsibility. It's simple to establish and has few legal requirements, but it offers no personal liability protection.
- **Partnership**: A business owned and managed by two or more individuals. It can be a general partnership (all partners have unlimited liability) or a limited partnership (only general partners have unlimited liability).
- **Limited Liability Company (LLC)**: A hybrid business structure that combines features of a corporation and a partnership. LLC owners (known as members) have limited

liability protection, meaning their personal assets are not at risk if the business is sued.
- **Corporation**: A separate legal entity from its owners (shareholders). It provides strong liability protection but comes with more complex legal and tax requirements.

2. Protecting Your Intellectual Property:

- **Patents**: A government-granted exclusive right to make, use, sell, or distribute an invention for a specific period. It's ideal for unique products or processes.
- **Trademarks**: A word, phrase, symbol, or design that identifies and distinguishes a product or service from others in the market. It protects your brand and prevents others from using similar marks.
- **Copyrights**: Protects original literary, artistic, and musical works from unauthorized use or reproduction. It's important for written works, music, artwork, and multimedia content.

3. Obtaining Permits and Licenses:

- Determine which permits and licenses are necessary for your business based on factors like location, industry, and specific activities.
- Common permits include health and safety permits (e.g., food handling permits), building permits (for construction or renovations), and environmental permits (for businesses that may impact the environment).
- Research and apply for the required licenses, such as business licenses (general operating licenses), professional licenses (for regulated professions like law or medicine), and sales tax permits (for businesses that sell taxable goods or services).

4. Understanding Contracts and Agreements:

- Carefully review and understand any contracts or agreements you enter into with customers, suppliers, partners, or employees.

- Ensure that the terms are clear and fair, and that you're fully aware of your rights and obligations.
- Consider seeking legal advice from an attorney if you're unsure about certain clauses or implications of a contract.

Remember, legal compliance is not just about avoiding trouble; it also establishes trust, professionalism, and a solid foundation for your business's growth and success in the long run.

COMING UP WITH A UNIQUE AND VIABLE BUSINESS IDEA

Finding a great business idea can be challenging, but it's an essential first step for aspiring entrepreneurs. Here are some strategies to help you generate and develop unique and viable business ideas:

1. Solve a Problem:

Start by thinking about the challenges and pain points you face in your own life or observe in your community. Is there a product or service that could solve these problems more effectively or conveniently? Identify problems that are widespread and have a significant impact on people's lives or businesses.

2. Follow Your Passion:

Consider turning your hobbies, interests, or passions into a business. If you're passionate about something, you're more likely to be motivated and dedicated to developing a successful business around it. Think about how you can monetize your skills, knowledge, or creativity.

3. Look for Trends:

Stay updated on the latest trends in technology, fashion, culture, and other industries. Identify emerging trends that have the potential to shape consumer behavior and create new market opportunities. Consider how you can capitalize on these trends by offering innovative products or services.

4. Brainstorm with Others:

Bounce ideas off friends, family, mentors, or fellow entrepreneurs. Sometimes, the best ideas come from collaboration and brainstorming sessions. Share your thoughts and concepts with others and gather their feedback. They may provide valuable insights or help you refine your ideas further.

5. Validate the Idea and Find the Target Market:

Once you have a business idea, it's important to validate it before investing significant resources. Here's how:

1. Market Research:

- Conduct market research to understand your target audience.
- Identify their demographics, psychographics, needs, wants, and pain points.
- Determine the size and growth potential of your target market.
- Analyze your competition and identify gaps or opportunities in the market.
- Estimate the demand for your product or service.

2. Surveys and Interviews:

- Talk to potential customers to get their feedback on your idea.
- Ask them if they would be interested in buying your product or service.
- Gather insights into their preferences, expectations, and willingness to pay.
- Use surveys and interviews to validate your assumptions

and gather valuable customer feedback.

3. Create a Prototype or MVP:

- Build a basic version of your product or service, known as a prototype or minimum viable product (MVP).
- Test the MVP with a small group of potential customers or early adopters.
- Gather feedback and iterate on your product or service based on the results of the testing.
- Use the MVP to validate your idea and refine your offering before launching it to a wider audience.

4. Build a Business Plan:

- Develop a comprehensive business plan that outlines your business goals, strategies, marketing plans, financial projections, and operational details.
- Use the business plan to attract investors, secure funding, and guide your business's growth and development.

5. Launch and Market Your Business:

- Once you have validated your idea, created a prototype, and developed a business plan, it's time to launch your business.
- Develop a marketing strategy to reach your target audience and generate awareness for your product or service.
- Use a combination of online and offline channels to promote your business, such as social media, email marketing, search engine optimization (SEO), content marketing, and public relations.

6. Monitor and Evaluate Your Business:

- Regularly monitor your business's performance and evaluate your progress.
- Track key metrics such as sales, revenue, customer acquisition cost, and customer churn rate.
- Make necessary adjustments to your business strategy based on the results of your evaluation.

- Continuously innovate and adapt to changing market conditions and customer needs.

Remember that starting a successful business takes hard work, dedication, and persistence. Be prepared to face challenges and setbacks along the way, but never give up on your vision.

By following these steps, you can increase your chances of launching a successful business, even if you're starting with limited resources. Remember, the most important thing is to take action and start building your dream.

MARKETING MANIA: GETTING YOUR BUSINESS NOTICED

Alright, you've got your business idea, you've honed your skills, and you're ready to take on the world. But how do you get the word out? How do you make sure your awesome product or service doesn't get lost in the vast sea of online content? Welcome to the world of marketing, where creativity, strategy, and a bit of hustle can make all the difference.

Social Media Marketing: Building a Following and Engaging Your Audience

Let's face it, you're probably already spending a good chunk of your time on social media. But are you using it to its full potential? Social media isn't just for scrolling through memes and stalking your crush; it's a powerful tool for building a community around your brand and attracting customers.

- **Choose Your Platforms Wisely:** Not all social media platforms are created equal. Focus on the platforms where your target audience hangs out. Are they on Instagram, TikTok, Twitter, or somewhere else?
- **Create Engaging Content:** Don't just post boring product photos or sales pitches. Share behind-the-scenes glimpses of your business, run contests and giveaways, and create content that sparks conversations and encourages interaction.

- **Use Hashtags Strategically:** Hashtags help people discover your content. Research relevant hashtags in your niche and use them in your posts.
- **Collaborate with Influencers:** Partnering with influencers in your niche can help you reach a wider audience and gain credibility.
- **Run Paid Ads:** If you have a budget, consider running targeted ads on social media platforms to reach a specific audience.

Content Creation: Creating Valuable Content That Attracts Customers

Content is king in the digital world. By creating valuable content that educates, entertains, or inspires your audience, you can attract potential customers and build trust with them.

- **Blog Posts:** Share your expertise, insights, and stories through blog posts. This can help you establish yourself as an authority in your field and drive traffic to your website.
- **Videos:** Create engaging videos that showcase your products or services, share tutorials, or tell your brand story. YouTube and TikTok are great platforms for sharing video content.
- **Podcasts:** If you're comfortable speaking, consider starting a podcast to share your knowledge and connect with your audience on a deeper level.
- **Infographics:** Visual content like infographics can be a great way to share information in an engaging and easy-to-digest format.

Paid Advertising: Using Online Ads to Reach a Wider Audience

While organic reach on social media is great, paid advertising can help you reach a much larger audience and target specific demographics.

- **Google Ads:** Pay to have your website appear at the top of

Google search results for relevant keywords.
- **Social Media Ads:** Run targeted ads on platforms like Facebook, Instagram, and Twitter to reach specific demographics and interests.
- **Display Ads:** Place banner ads on websites that your target audience frequents.
- **Retargeting Ads:** Show ads to people who have previously visited your website or interacted with your brand on social media.

NETWORKING AND PARTNERSHIPS: COLLABORATING WITH OTHERS TO GROW YOUR BUSINESS

Networking and collaboration are vital strategies for entrepreneurs seeking to accelerate their business growth. By building relationships with other entrepreneurs, influencers, and businesses in your niche, you can unlock a world of opportunities and propel your venture forward.

Here are some effective ways to leverage the power of networking and partnerships:

1. Attend Industry Events:
- Participate in conferences, trade shows, meetups, and networking events related to your industry.
- Prepare an elevator pitch to introduce yourself and your business confidently.
- Collect business cards and connect with attendees on LinkedIn afterwards.

2. Join Online Communities:

- Engage in online forums, groups, and communities dedicated to your niche.
- Share valuable insights, answer questions, and establish yourself as a thought leader.
- Collaborate with other members on projects or initiatives.

3. Collaborate on Projects:

- Seek out opportunities to partner with other businesses or influencers on projects that align with your goals.
- Co-host webinars, create joint content, or launch cross-promotions.
- Leverage each other's networks and resources for mutual benefit.

4. Offer Affiliate Programs:

- Implement an affiliate program to encourage others to promote your products or services.
- Provide attractive commission rates and marketing materials to facilitate their efforts.
- Track and reward affiliates based on their performance.

5. Build Strategic Partnerships:

- Identify businesses that complement your offerings and explore partnership possibilities.
- Collaborate on product development, distribution, or marketing initiatives.
- Jointly target new markets or customer segments.

6. Attend Local Business Networking Events:

- Attend events such as Chamber of Commerce mixers or industry-specific networking events.
- Participate in local business organizations and volunteer opportunities.
- Connect with other entrepreneurs and professionals in your

community.

7. Leverage Social Media Platforms:

- Engage with influencers, thought leaders, and potential customers on social media.
- Share valuable content, interact with followers, and build a strong online presence.
- Utilize social media platforms to initiate conversations and foster relationships.

8. Join Professional Organizations:

- Become a member of professional organizations related to your industry or field.
- Attend meetings, workshops, and events organized by these organizations.
- Network with peers and explore opportunities for collaboration.

By actively networking and cultivating strategic partnerships, you can expand your reach, gain credibility, and accelerate the growth of your business. Remember to approach networking with a genuine interest in building mutually beneficial relationships, and always be open to new opportunities and collaborations.

MARKETING THE BUSINESS EFFECTIVELY

Effective marketing is crucial for businesses to succeed in today's competitive market. It involves understanding the target audience, crafting compelling messages, selecting appropriate channels, and tracking results to refine strategies.

Defining the Target Audience:

- Identify the ideal customer.
- Conduct market research to gather insights into demographics, psychographics, and behavior.
- Segment the target audience based on specific characteristics to tailor marketing messages.

Developing a Unique Selling Proposition (USP):

- Differentiate the business from competitors by identifying unique features, benefits, and value propositions.
- Clearly articulate the USP in all marketing communications.

Creating a Marketing Plan:

- Set specific, measurable, achievable, relevant, and time-bound (SMART) marketing goals.
- Develop marketing strategies aligned with business objectives.
- Outline tactics for each strategy, including channels, content, and promotional activities.

- Allocate resources effectively to maximize impact.

Tracking and Analyzing Results:

- Implement analytics tools to monitor website traffic, conversions, and customer engagement.
- Regularly evaluate marketing campaigns to determine their effectiveness.
- Analyze data to identify trends, patterns, and areas for improvement.
- Make data-driven decisions to optimize marketing efforts.

Reaching the Target Audience and Generating Leads:

- Content Marketing:
  - Create high-quality, informative, and engaging content that resonates with the target audience.
  - Publish content consistently on the company's website, blog, and social media platforms.
  - Promote content through email marketing, social media, and paid advertising.
- Social Media Marketing:
  - Establish a strong presence on relevant social media platforms.
  - Engage with followers through posts, comments, and direct messages.
  - Use social media advertising to reach a wider audience and generate leads.
- Paid Advertising:
  - Identify the right advertising platforms based on the target audience and campaign goals.
  - Develop targeted ad campaigns with compelling visuals and persuasive copy.
  - Monitor ad performance and adjust strategies accordingly.
- Email Marketing:
  - Build an email list by offering valuable content, incentives, or exclusive offers.

- o   Create personalized email campaigns that provide relevant information and promote products or services.
- o   Automate email sequences to nurture leads and build relationships.

Building an Online Presence and Social Media Strategy

Your online presence is your digital storefront. It's how potential customers will find and interact with your brand.

- **Website:** Create a professional website that showcases your products or services, tells your brand story, and makes it easy for customers to contact you.
- **Social Media:** Build a strong presence on social media platforms where your target audience hangs out.
- **Online Directories:** List your business in online directories like Google My Business and Yelp.
- **Review Sites:** Encourage customers to leave reviews on platforms like Google and Facebook.

By mastering these marketing strategies and tactics, you can get your business noticed, attract more customers, and achieve your entrepreneurial goals.

THE COLLEGE DILEMMA: IS IT THE RIGHT PATH FOR YOU?

- What are your passions and interests? Will college help you pursue them?
- What kind of career do you envision for yourself? Does it require a degree?
- Are you willing to take on student loan debt? If so, how much?
- Are you self-motivated and disciplined enough to succeed in an alternative learning environment?

By honestly answering these questions, you can make an informed decision about whether college is the right path for you. Remember, there's no shame in choosing a different route if it aligns better with your goals and values.

In today's rapidly changing job market, a traditional college education is not always the most suitable or necessary path to success. Alternative education options, such as coding boot camps, online courses, and apprenticeships, have emerged as viable alternatives for many individuals.

- **Coding Bootcamps:**
  Coding boot camps are intensive, short-term programs that teach in-demand coding skills. These boot camps often last from a few weeks to a few months and provide a practical

and hands-on approach to learning programming languages, frameworks, and software development techniques. They are particularly suited for individuals looking to make a career change or those aiming to acquire specific programming skills quickly. Coding boot camps can be a fast track to a lucrative career in tech, with some graduates securing high-paying jobs after completing their programs.

- **Online Courses:**
Online courses offer a flexible and convenient way to learn new skills and enhance existing knowledge. Platforms like Coursera, Udemy, Skillshare, and edX provide a vast array of courses on various subjects, including programming, business, design, and more. Online courses can be taken at one's own pace, often at a fraction of the cost of traditional education. They are ideal for individuals who want to learn new skills on their own time, those who live in remote areas, and those who have busy schedules.

- **Apprenticeships:**
Apprenticeships combine hands-on work experience with formal training, allowing individuals to learn from seasoned professionals in their field of interest. Apprentices work under the supervision of a mentor or master, gaining practical skills and knowledge while receiving a salary. Apprenticeships are particularly beneficial for individuals who prefer a more hands-on approach to learning and those who want to build their skills while earning an income. They are also a great way to network and build connections in a particular industry.

Alternative education options, such as coding boot camps, online courses, and apprenticeships, offer several advantages over traditional college education. They are often more affordable, flexible, and tailored to specific career goals. They provide individuals with the skills and knowledge needed to succeed in today's job market and pave the way for a successful and fulfilling career.

BUILDING YOUR BUSINESS WHILE IN SCHOOL: BALANCING EDUCATION AND ENTREPRENEURSHIP

Combining education and entrepreneurship is an ambitious endeavor that requires careful planning, effective time management, and unwavering dedication. While it may seem daunting, it's definitely achievable with the right strategies. Here are some expanded tips to help you navigate this challenging but rewarding path:

1. Prioritize Your Activities:

- Identify the most critical tasks for your business and academic success. Create a to-do list and prioritize these activities.
- Focus your time and energy on high-priority tasks and avoid distractions.
- Use the Eisenhower Matrix to categorize tasks based on urgency and importance.

2. Delegate and Outsource:

- Don't try to be a one-person show. Delegate tasks to capable individuals or outsource them to freelancers or external

providers.
- Identify tasks that can be delegated without compromising quality, such as administrative tasks, social media management, or graphic design.
- Consider outsourcing tasks that require specialized skills or knowledge.

3. Set Realistic Goals:

- Avoid setting yourself up for failure by setting unrealistic goals.
- Break down your business and academic goals into smaller, achievable milestones.
- Focus on one goal at a time and celebrate your progress as you reach each milestone.

4. Take Advantage of Resources:

- Many colleges and universities offer resources specifically designed for student entrepreneurs.
- Explore incubators, co-working spaces, and mentorship programs offered by your institution.
- Participate in entrepreneurship competitions and networking events to connect with like-minded individuals.

5. Stay Organized and Efficient:

- Use productivity tools and techniques to manage your time effectively.
- Create a dedicated workspace that's conducive to focus and creativity.
- Plan your day in advance and stick to your schedule as much as possible.

6. Maintain a Healthy Balance:

- While it's important to work hard, don't neglect your physical and mental well-being.
- Make time for exercise, relaxation, and social activities.
- Set boundaries between your work and personal life to avoid

burnout.

7. Seek Support and Guidance:

- Don't hesitate to reach out for help when needed.
- Talk to professors, advisors, or experienced entrepreneurs for guidance and support.
- Join entrepreneurship communities and networks to connect with others pursuing similar goals.

Remember, building a business while in school is a marathon, not a sprint. Stay persistent, adaptable, and open to learning from your experiences. With dedication and hard work, you can achieve your entrepreneurial aspirations while also excelling in your studies.

Giving Back: Making a Difference with Your Wealth

Financial freedom isn't just about accumulating wealth for yourself; it's also about using your resources to make a positive impact on the world. As a young entrepreneur, you have the power to create a business that not only generates income but also contributes to a greater good.

Young Philanthropists: Inspiring Stories of Young People Making an Impact

You might be surprised to learn that many young people are already making a significant difference in the world through philanthropy and social entrepreneurship.

- **Ryan Hickman:** Started a recycling business at age 3 and has since recycled over 1 million plastic bottles.
- **Katie Stagliano:** Founded a nonprofit organization at age 9 that grows fresh produce for people in need.
- **Xiuhtezcatl Martinez:** A young environmental activist who has spoken at the United Nations and is fighting for climate justice.

These young changemakers prove that you don't have to wait until you're older to make a difference. You can start now, using your entrepreneurial skills and passion to create a positive impact on your community and the world.

Social Entrepreneurship: Building a Business That Solves Social Problems

Social entrepreneurship is a growing movement that combines business with a social mission. It's about creating businesses that not only generate profit but also address social or environmental challenges.

- **Identify a Problem:** What social or environmental issues are you passionate about? Is there a way to create a business that addresses these issues?
- **Develop a Solution:** Create a product or service that solves the problem you've identified.
- **Measure Your Impact:** Track the social or environmental impact of your business. How many lives have you touched? How much waste have you reduced?

Leaving a Legacy: How to Use Your Wealth to Create a Lasting Impact

Building a legacy is about more than just leaving money behind. It's about creating something that will outlive you and continue to make a difference in the world.

- **Charitable Giving:** Donate to causes you care about. You can start small and increase your contributions as your wealth grows.
- **Invest in Education:** Support educational initiatives that empower young people and provide them with the skills they need to succeed.
- **Start a Foundation:** If you have significant wealth, consider

starting a foundation to support your philanthropic goals.
- **Mentor Others:** Share your knowledge and experience with aspiring entrepreneurs. Help them achieve their dreams and make a positive impact on the world.

Making a Positive Social Impact with Your Business

Even if you're not a social entrepreneur, you can still make a positive social impact with your business.

- **Support Local Charities:** Donate a portion of your profits to local charities or organizations that are making a difference in your community.
- **Partner with Nonprofits:** Collaborate with nonprofits on projects that align with your values and mission.
- **Offer Pro Bono Services:** Donate your time and expertise to help those in need.
- **Promote Sustainability:** Implement sustainable practices in your business operations to minimize your environmental impact.

Balancing Profit with Ethical Considerations

As a young entrepreneur, it's important to balance your desire for profit with ethical considerations.

- **Transparency:** Be transparent about your business practices and pricing.
- **Fairness:** Treat your employees, customers, and suppliers fairly and with respect.
- **Social Responsibility:** Consider the social and environmental impact of your business decisions.
- **Give Back:** Donate a portion of your profits to charitable causes or organizations that are making a difference in the world.

By incorporating social responsibility into your business model, you can create a company that not only generates wealth but also contributes to a better world.

In the digital era, education has transcended the confines of traditional classrooms, and online learning platforms have emerged as powerful tools for young entrepreneurs. These platforms offer a wealth of resources to facilitate learning, knowledge expansion, and networking opportunities.

Online Learning Platforms: Your Classroom Without Walls
In this chapter, we embark on a journey through the realm of online learning platforms, exploring the vast array of opportunities available to young entrepreneurs. From Massive Open Online Courses (MOOCs) to skill-specific platforms, mentorship and coaching programs, and a guide to finding the right mentors and resources, this chapter provides a comprehensive overview of the digital landscape of education.

Massive Open Online Courses (MOOCs): Free or Low-Cost Courses from Top Universities
MOOCs have revolutionized access to higher education, allowing learners from all walks of life to enroll in courses offered by prestigious universities worldwide. These courses cover a wide spectrum of subjects, enabling individuals to explore new fields, enhance their existing knowledge, and gain valuable skills. Platforms such as Coursera, edX, Udemy, and Khan Academy offer a diverse range of MOOCs, many of which are free or very affordable.

Skill-Specific Platforms: Learning Coding, Design, Marketing, and More
For those seeking to develop specific skills in areas such as coding, design, marketing, and beyond, there are numerous online platforms catering to different interests. Codecademy provides an interactive learning environment for aspiring coders, while Skillshare offers creative courses in graphic design, illustration,

and photography. General Assembly focuses on web development, data science, and digital marketing, and HubSpot Academy provides free certifications in inbound marketing, sales, and customer service.

Mentorship and Coaching Programs: Personalized Guidance and Support

Mentorship and coaching programs offer invaluable guidance, support, and accountability to young entrepreneurs. Working directly with experienced individuals who have achieved success in their respective fields can accelerate learning and provide tailored advice. Organizations such as SCORE, MicroMentor, and The Founder Institute connect entrepreneurs with seasoned mentors who can offer insights, strategies, and encouragement.

Finding the Right Mentors and Resources: Unlocking Your Potential

Finding the right mentors and resources can have a transformative impact on an entrepreneur's journey. Mentors can provide invaluable advice, guidance, and support, while resources can equip individuals with the tools and knowledge necessary for success. Networking, attending industry events, joining online communities, and researching organizations that support young entrepreneurs are effective ways to identify potential mentors and resources.

Be Proactive: Seizing Opportunities and Taking Action

Entrepreneurs who take a proactive approach to their learning and development are more likely to succeed. Reaching out to potential mentors, asking for advice, and actively seeking out opportunities for growth are essential steps in unlocking one's full potential. By embracing online learning platforms, connecting with mentors, and utilizing available resources, young entrepreneurs can navigate the challenges of entrepreneurship with confidence and a solid foundation for success.

TECH TOOLS FOR YOUNG HUSTLERS

In today's digital landscape, technology is your best friend. There are countless tools and platforms available to help you build your online presence, manage your business, and connect with customers.

Website Builders and E-commerce Platforms: Creating Your Online Presence

Your website is your digital storefront, so make sure it's a good one. Website builders like Wix, Squarespace, and Shopify make it easy to create a professional-looking website without any coding knowledge.

- **Wix:** Offers a drag-and-drop interface and a wide range of templates to choose from.
- **Squarespace:** Known for its sleek and modern designs.
- **Shopify:** A popular e-commerce platform for selling products online.

Social Media Management Tools: Scheduling Posts, Analyzing Data, and Engaging with Your Audience

Managing multiple social media accounts can be a time-consuming task. Social media management tools like Hootsuite, Buffer, and Sprout Social can help you schedule posts, track your analytics, and engage with your audience more efficiently.

- **Hootsuite:** Allows you to manage multiple social media accounts from one dashboard.
- **Buffer:** Simplifies social media scheduling and provides analytics to track your performance.
- **Sprout Social:** Offers a comprehensive suite of social media management tools, including listening, publishing, and analytics.

Financial Tracking and Budgeting Apps: Managing Your Money Like a Pro

Keeping track of your finances is crucial for any entrepreneur. Financial tracking and budgeting apps like Mint, YNAB (You Need a Budget), and Personal Capital can help you track your income and expenses, create budgets, and set financial goals.

- **Mint:** A popular budgeting app that automatically tracks your spending and categorizes your transactions.
- **YNAB:** A budgeting system that helps you give every dollar a job and gain control of your finances.
- **Personal Capital:** A comprehensive financial tool that tracks your investments, net worth, and retirement savings.

Building a Website or Online Store

Your website is your online home base, so make sure it's a good one. If you're selling products online, you'll need an e-commerce platform that allows you to showcase your products, process payments, and manage your inventory.

- **Shopify:** A popular e-commerce platform that's easy to use and offers a wide range of features.
- **WooCommerce:** A customizable e-commerce plugin for WordPress.
- **BigCommerce:** A scalable e-commerce platform for growing businesses.

CHOOSING THE RIGHT TECHNOLOGY TOOLS AND PLATFORMS

The right technology tools can streamline your business operations, save you time, and help you reach more customers. But with so many options available, it can be overwhelming to choose the right ones.

Do Your Research: Before investing in any tool or platform, do your research to make sure it's the right fit for your business. Read reviews, compare features, and consider your budget.

Start with the Essentials: Don't try to use every tool under the sun. Start with the essentials, such as a website builder, social media management tool, and financial tracking app.

Experiment and Iterate: Don't be afraid to try new tools and platforms. As your business grows, your needs will change, so be prepared to adapt and evolve your tech stack.

Building a sustainable business model involves creating a framework that ensures long-term viability and profitability. It goes beyond short-term gains and emphasizes the ability of a business to thrive over an extended period. Here's an expanded exploration of the key elements of a sustainable business model:

1. Recurring Revenue:

- Establish subscription-based services or membership programs to generate predictable cash flow.
- Offer ongoing support, updates, or exclusive content to retain subscribers over time.

2. Diversification:

- Develop a diverse product or service portfolio to reduce reliance on a single offering.
- Target multiple customer segments or markets to mitigate risk and increase growth opportunities.

3. Customer Retention:

- Prioritize excellent customer service to foster loyalty and repeat business.
- Implement customer loyalty programs, personalized experiences, and post-purchase engagement strategies.

4. Cost Management:

- Optimize operational efficiency to minimize expenses and maximize profits.
- Leverage technology, automation, and outsourcing to streamline processes and reduce costs.

5. Adaptability:

- Continuously monitor market trends and customer feedback to identify opportunities and challenges.
- Maintain a flexible business model that can pivot quickly in response to changing circumstances.

6. Sustainability:

- Integrate environmentally friendly practices into your business operations and supply chain.
- Offer products or services that align with ethical and sustainable values to attract conscious consumers.

7. Innovation:

- Invest in research and development to create innovative products, services, or processes.
- Encourage a culture of creativity and experimentation to stay ahead of the competition.

8. Strong Leadership:

- Cultivate a visionary and inspiring leadership team that can effectively guide the organization towards sustainable growth.
- Foster a collaborative and empowering work environment to unleash the potential of employees.

9. Financial Planning:

- Develop a comprehensive financial plan that outlines revenue projections, cost estimates, and investment requirements.
- Regularly monitor financial performance and make necessary adjustments to ensure financial stability.

10. Stakeholder Engagement:

- Establish open communication channels with stakeholders, including investors, employees, and customers.
- Seek feedback, address concerns, and maintain transparency to build trust and support.

By implementing these strategies and continuously adapting to evolving market conditions, businesses can establish a sustainable business model that ensures long-term success and resilience.

APPENDIX: ADDITIONAL RESOURCES FOR YOUNG ENTREPRENEURS

A1: Recommended Books

- *Rich Dad Poor Dad* by Robert Kiyosaki
- *The Lean Startup* by Eric Ries
- *Zero to One* by Peter Thiel
- *The 4-Hour Workweek* by Tim Ferriss
- *Crushing It!* by Gary Vaynerchuk

A2: Online Communities and Forums

- **Young Entrepreneur Council (YEC):** A community of successful young entrepreneurs who share advice and support.
- **Startup Nation:** A forum for entrepreneurs of all ages to connect and share resources.
- **Reddit Entrepreneurs:** A subreddit where entrepreneurs discuss business ideas, challenges, and successes.

A3: Government Resources

- **Small Business Administration (SBA):** Offers resources and support for small businesses, including loans, counseling, and training programs.
- **SCORE:** A nonprofit organization that provides free mentoring and counseling to entrepreneurs.

A4: Financial Tools and Resources

- **Mint:** A popular budgeting app that helps you track your income and expenses.
- **YNAB (You Need a Budget):** A budgeting system that helps you give every dollar a job.
- **Acorns:** An app that rounds up your purchases and invests the spare change.
- **Robinhood:** A commission-free investing app that makes it easy to buy and sell stocks and cryptocurrencies.

CONCLUSION: YOUR JOURNEY TO FINANCIAL FREEDOM STARTS NOW

Congratulations! You've now been equipped with the knowledge, skills, and resources to embark on your entrepreneurial journey. Remember, the path to financial freedom is not always easy, but it's definitely worth it.

Embrace your youth, your creativity, and your passion. Don't be afraid to take risks, learn from your mistakes, and never give up on your dreams. The world is yours for the taking.

So what are you waiting for? Start building your empire today!

DISCLAIMER

The information presented in this book is intended to provide a general overview of the field of digital public relations and its best practices. While every effort has been made to ensure the accuracy and timeliness of the information, the digital landscape is constantly evolving. As such, some statistics, platform features, and industry trends may have changed since the time of publication.

The reader is encouraged to cross-reference information with current industry reports and to consult multiple sources for a comprehensive understanding. The strategies, tactics, and examples provided are for illustrative purposes only, and should be adapted and applied to each reader's unique context and goals.

The author and publisher make no warranties, express or implied, regarding the completeness, accuracy, or suitability of the information presented. The reader assumes full responsibility for the use and application of this information, and the author and publisher disclaim any liability for any losses or damages arising from its use.

Other works by Kim Domingo Reyes
https://hi.switchy.io/kimdomingoreyes

www.ingramcontent.com/pod-product-compliance
Lightning Source LLC
Chambersburg PA
CBHW030501220526
45464CB00006B/2610